This book belongs to:

....

..Laila..............................

Written by Moira Butterfield
Illustrated by Rachael O'Neill

This edition published by Parragon Books Ltd in 2015
and distributed by

Parragon Inc.
440 Park Avenue South, 13th Floor
New York, NY 10016
www.parragon.com

ISBN 978-1-4748-0339-7

Printed in China

I'm Sorry!

PaRRagon

Bath • New York • Cologne • Melbourne • Delhi
Hong Kong • Shenzhen • Singapore • Amsterdam

Mind your child's manners!

It's important to start teaching good manners early so that they become a habit for life. The stories in the MIND YOUR MANNERS! series are written to make learning good manners a positive experience.

Here are some of the ways you can help to make it fun:

* Find a quiet time to look at this story together and encourage your child to join in. The rhymes make the story easy to remember.

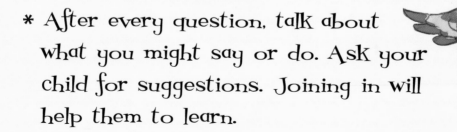

* After every question, talk about what you might say or do. Ask your child for suggestions. Joining in will help them to learn.

* Use the pages at the end of the story to check that your child understands when it is appropriate to use good manners. There's a reward star for every right answer.

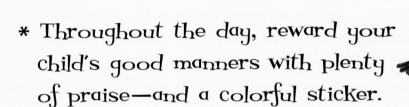

* Throughout the day, reward your child's good manners with plenty of praise—and a colorful sticker.

What naughty monkeys
at the zoo!
They're dropping their food
and throwing it, too.

The monkeys don't speak, but if they could, they should say sorry for not being good.

If you drop your food
like the monkeys do. . .

. . . What should you say?

Say "I'm sorry!" too.

What noisy hippos at the zoo!
They've woken the sleepy old gnu.

The hippos don't speak,
but if they could,
they should say sorry
for not being good.

If you make a noisy hullabaloo. . .

...What should you say?

Say "I'm sorry!" too.

What silly penguins at the zoo!
They're splashing the lions
and the tigers, too.

The penguins don't speak, but if they could, they should say sorry for not being good.

If you splash your friends when you shouldn't do. . .

. . .What should you say?

Say "I'm sorry!" too.

What grumpy zebras at the zoo!
They're pushing in front of the
kangaroo.

The zebras don't speak,
but if they could,
they should say sorry
for not being good!

If you push someone like the zebras do. . .

. . .What should you say?

Say "I'm sorry!" too.

None of the animals in the zoo
know good manners like you do.

But just imagine
if they could. . .
What should they say
for not being good?

"Sorry!"

What will you say?

If you drop your food,
what should you say?

If you said "I'm sorry," you were right!

If you make too much noise,
what should you say?

If you said "I'm sorry," you were right!

Did you say "Sorry"
in all the right places?
Then give yourself four stars!

If you make someone angry, what should you say?

If you said "I'm sorry," you were right!

If you bump into someone, what should you say?

If you said "I'm sorry," you were right!